HOPSCOTCH
TWISTY TALES

Too Many Nightingales!

by Sam Hay and Roger Simó

W
FRANKLIN WATTS

This story is based on the traditional fairy tale,
The Nightingale, but with a new twist.
Can you make up your own twist for the story?

Franklin Watts
First published in Great Britain in 2016 by The Watts Publishing Group

Text © Sam Hay 2016
Illustrations © Roger Simó 2016

ISBN 978 1 4451 4755 0 (hbk)
ISBN 978 1 4451 4756 7 (pbk)
ISBN 978 1 4451 4757 4 (library ebook)

Series Editor: Melanie Palmer
Series Advisor: Catherine Glavina
Series Designer: Peter Scoulding
Cover Designer: Cathryn Gilbert

Printed in China

Franklin Watts
An imprint of
Hachette Children's Group
Part of The Watts Publishing Group
Carmelite House
50 Victoria Embankment
London EC4Y 0DZ

An Hachette UK Company
www.hachette.co.uk

www.franklinwatts.co.uk

Once upon a throne, there was a
very trendy young king and
queen who liked to wear the
coolest clothes and have all the
latest gadgets.

The people in the kingdom loved reading about the royal couple ...

and whatever the king and queen
did, the people did too!

Then, one day, a nightingale
flew into the palace garden.
"What a lovely sound," said
the king.

"Such a pretty bird," said the queen. "I do hope it doesn't fly away!"

"We'll build it a bird table," said the king.

"And feed it every day!" said the queen. "Then it will stay in our garden forever."

Soon, everyone was talking about the king and queen's love for the nightingale.

Because the king and queen loved the bird, everyone else did, too! The kingdom went nightingale nuts!

Pictures of the bird appeared on everything, from hats and T-shirts to plates and pants.

There were nightingale cuckoo clocks and nightingale teapots. Some people even named their children 'Nightingale'!

Of course, everyone wanted a real
nightingale, just like the king's.
But there weren't enough birds to
go around.

Then, one day, a toy maker
had a clever idea.

"Clockwork nightingales!" she
said. "That's what I'll make!"

Word spread quickly. People came from all around to buy the little wind-up birds that would tweet for hours.

The royal couple were not amused!
"What a din!" cried the king.

"Such a racket!" wailed the queen. But no one could hear them over the noise of the birds.

19

The real nightingale was so scared
by the clockwork tweeting,
it flew away.

The king and queen sat in their garden with their fingers in their ears feeling very fed-up indeed, until, one day, a stranger appeared.

"My name's Hamelin," he said. "I'll fix your problem!" He pulled out a bird-shaped flute and began to play a beautiful tune.

The wind blew, the trees swayed,
and suddenly there was the sound
of metal wings flapping.
From all over the kingdom the
clockwork nightingales appeared.

Hamelin set off out of the town, still playing his flute, with the toy birds following him.

As soon as the clockwork birds left,
the real nightingale returned.

The pipe-playing man called
Hamelin returned, too.
"I left the birds in a forest far
away," he explained.

"Thanks!" said the king.
"Before you go, could I try your
flute? I've always wanted to learn
to play an instrument."
"Me, too!" said the queen.

Soon the kingdom was full of noise again. The nightingale flew off for good this time.

But no one cared. Not even the king and queen. They were all too busy rocking!

Put these pictures in the correct order.
Which event do you think is most important?
Now try writing the story in your own words!

Puzzle 2

Choose the correct speech bubbles for each character. Can you think of any others? Turn over to find the answers.

Answers

Puzzle 1

The correct order is: 1c, 2f, 3d, 4e, 5a, 6b

Puzzle 2

The king and queen: 2, 5

The nightingale: 1, 4

Hamelin: 3, 6

Look out for more Hopscotch Twisty Tales

The Ninjabread Man
ISBN 978 1 4451 3964 7
The Boy Who Cried Sheep!
ISBN 978 1 4451 4292 0
Thumbelina Thinks Big
ISBN 978 1 4451 4295 1
**Move versus the
Enormous Turnip**
ISBN 978 1 4451 4300 2
Big Pancacke to the Rescue
ISBN 978 1 4451 4303 3
Little Red Hen's Great Escape
ISBN 978 1 4451 4305 7
The Lovely Duckling
ISBN 978 1 4451 1633 4
**Hansel and Gretel
and the Green Witch**
ISBN 978 1 4451 1634 1
The Emperor's New Kit
ISBN 978 1 4451 1635 8

**Rapunzel and the
Prince of Pop**
ISBN 978 1 4451 1636 5
**Dick Whittington
Gets on his Bike**
ISBN 978 1 4451 1637 2
**The Pied Piper and
the Wrong Song**
ISBN 978 1 4451 1638 9
**The Princess and the
Frozen Peas**
ISBN 978 1 4451 0675 5
Snow White Sees the Light
ISBN 978 1 4451 0676 2
**The Elves and the
Trendy Shoes**
ISBN 978 1 4451 0678 6
The Three Frilly Goats Fluff
ISBN 978 1 4451 0677 9

Princess Frog
ISBN 978 1 4451 0679 3
Rumpled Stilton Skin
ISBN 978 1 4451 0680 9
Jack and the Bean Pie
ISBN 978 1 4451 0182 8
**Brownilocks and the Three Bowls
of Cornflakes**
ISBN 978 1 4451 0183 5
Cinderella's Big Foot
ISBN 978 1 4451 0184 2
Little Bad Riding Hood
ISBN 978 1 4451 0185 9
**Sleeping Beauty –
100 Years Later**
ISBN 978 1 4451 0186 6
**The Three Little Pigs &
the New Neighbour**
ISBN 978 1 4451 0181 1

For more Hopscotch books go to:
www.franklinwatts.co.uk